How Crab got his Claws

by Rudyard Kipling

Illustrated by John Joven

Retold by Rosie Dickins

Reading consultant: Alison Kelly

Once, Crab was huge
and he had no claws.

This story tells how
that changed.

In the beginning

the Wise Man told the
animals how to behave.

He told every animal.

Crab ran away.

The other animals
played nicely.

Crab did NOT...

When Crab played,
the sea flooded...

SPLASH!

or turned to mud!

"WHO is doing that?"
asked the Wise Man.

"Not us," said
the animals.

"What about Crab?"
said a girl.

"He ran away
when you were
talking."

"Crab," called the Wise Man. "Stop playing with the sea!"

"Ha, ha. NO!"
shouted Crab.

"I'll do magic," warned the Wise Man.

Crab didn't care.

"I'm so small!" wailed Crab. "How will I eat?"

"I'll give you my scissors," said the girl.

"Then you can crack shells and eat nuts."

Crab took them.

Now *all* crabs have scissor-claws – and some really do eat nuts.

PUZZLES

Puzzle 1

Complete the sentence.

_____ did what he wanted.

Cow

Turtle

Crab

Puzzle 2

Put the pictures in order.

A

The Wise Man did magic.

B

Crab shrank.

C

Crab was very big.

Puzzle 3
True or False?

Crab ran away.

Crab played nicely.

Crab got bigger.

Puzzle 4

Spot five differences
between the two pictures.

Answers to puzzles

Puzzle 1

<u>Crab</u> did what he wanted.

Puzzle 2

C   Crab was very big.

A   The Wise Man did magic.

B   Crab shrank.

Puzzle 3

Crab
ran away.
True

Crab played
nicely.
False

Crab got bigger.
False

Puzzle 4

About the story

This story is from the book *Just So Stories* by Rudyard Kipling, which tells how animals came to be the way they are.

Designed by Laura Nelson Norris
Series designer: Russell Punter
Series editor: Lesley Sims

This edition first published in 2019 by Usborne Publishing Ltd., Usborne House, 83-85 Saffron Hill, London EC1N 8RT, England. www.usborne.com Copyright © 2019, 2018 Usborne Publishing Ltd.

UE. First published in America in 2019. EDC, Tulsa, Oklahoma 74146 www.usbornebooksandmore.com
Library of Congress Control Number: 2019945364